OAKLEY

Europe

SANDRA NEWMAN

Children's Press®
An Imprint of Scholastic Inc.
New York Toronto London Auckland Sydney
Kong
Danbury, Connecticut

Content Consultant
Martin Schain
Professor of Politics
New York University
New York, NY

Library of Congress Cataloging-in-Publication Data

Newman, Sandra, 1965-
  Europe / by Sandra Newman.
    p. cm. -- (A true book)
  Includes index.
      ISBN-13: 978-0-531-16867-7 (lib. bdg.)
              978-0-531-21829-7 (pbk.)
      ISBN-10: 0-531-16867-0 (lib. bdg.)
              0-531-21829-5 (pbk.)

  1. Europe--Geography--Juvenile literature. I. Title. II. Series.

  D900. N48 2008
  940--dc22   2008000651

Produced by Weldon Owen Education Inc.

©2009 Scholastic Inc.

Find the Truth!

Everything you are about to read is true *except* for one of the sentences on this page.

Which one is **TRUE**?

T or F   Europe's birthrate is increasing rapidly.

T or F   In Venice, Italy, canals take the place of some streets.

Find the answers in this book.

3

Contents

THE BIG TRUTH!

Country in a City

Ireland and Iceland have no snakes.

Norway is in northern Europe. It has many fjords. These are long, narrow inlets of sea that form harbors along the coastline.

CHAPTER 1

Plenty to Offer

Europe has a great variety of people and places. It is the second smallest continent—only Australia is smaller. It covers only 4,037,000 square miles (10,456,000 square kilometers). That's not much larger than the United States. Yet Europe includes 48 countries. It has fjords (FYORDS) and glaciers in the north, the towering Alps in the center, and sun-drenched islands in the south.

Fjords are formed when glaciers shrink. The empty space left behind fills with seawater.

Svalbard (Norway)

Europe

Barents Sea

Norwegian Sea

Iceland

Sweden   Finland

Baltic
Sea

Norway

Estonia

Latvia

Russia

Denmark

Lithuania

North
Sea

United
Kingdom

1   Germany

Ireland

Poland

Belarus

English Channel

2   Czech
     Republic

France

Ukraine

Kazakhstan

Slovakia

North Atlantic Ocean

3

4   Austria

Hungary

19

Caspian
Sea

5   11   Romania

12

Adriatic Sea

13   14

6   7   8

Bulgaria   Black Sea

Georgia

9   Italy

15   16

17   18

Turkey

Azerbaijan

Portugal

Spain

Greece

Mediterranean Sea

10   Aegean Sea

Ionian Sea

ASIA

AFRICA

Gulf Stream

Key to Numbered Countries

1 The Netherlands	6 Andorra	11 Slovenia	15 Montenegro
2 Belgium	7 Monaco	12 Croatia	16 Kosovo
3 Luxembourg	8 San Marino	13 Bosnia and	17 Albania
4 Liechtenstein	9 Vatican City	Herzegovina	18 Macedonia
5 Switzerland	10 Malta	14 Serbia	19 Moldova

—— Country border

▪▪▪▪ Border between Europe and Asia (Turkey, Azerbaijan, Georgia,
Kazakhstan, and Russia have land in both continents)

〰 Ural Mountains

Cool and Warm

Europe is located entirely in the northern hemisphere. The farther north you go, the colder it gets. Parts of Spain, Italy, and Greece, in the south, have a mild climate. Winters in the United Kingdom and Ireland, and along the coast of Norway, are less severe than usual for those **latitudes**. This is because of the Gulf Stream, a powerful and warm current that runs like a river through the Atlantic Ocean. Winds warmed by the current blow along the west coast of the continent.

Because of the Gulf Stream, southern Spain is as warm as Florida. However, it is as far north as Colorado!

Keeping Dry

One part of Europe, the Netherlands, is known for its flatness. The Netherlands is on the western edge of the continent, next to the North Sea. About a quarter of the land is below sea level. The Dutch have kept their heads above water, though, by building dikes, or levees. These are thick, earthen walls that hold back the seawater. Any water that does seep into land areas is drained off into **canals**.

In the Netherlands, water is pumped out to sea through canals. In the past, windmills powered the pumps.

In Venice, many "streets" are made of water.

Life by the Water

Many of the cities of Europe were built on the banks of rivers or next to the sea. That's because before the invention of cars and trucks, the fastest way to transport things was by boat. One particularly watery city is Venice, in Italy. Venice is built on about 120 islands in the Adriatic Sea. Canals take the place of many streets, and boats replace cars.

The entire country of Monaco would fit inside New York City's Central Park. Monaco is less than one square mile (two square kilometers) in size.

Tiny States

Europe has some large countries, such as France and Germany. It also has tiny countries. These are often called "microstates." The smallest is Vatican City, which is found within the city of Rome in Italy. You could walk across Vatican City in only 10 minutes! About 1,000 people live there. Other microstates are Andorra, Liechtenstein, Luxembourg, Malta, Monaco, and San Marino.

Good-bye, Europe! Hello, Asia!

There is no clear geographical border between Europe and Asia. They are part of one landmass, called Eurasia. Russia is one of several countries that have parts in both Europe and Asia. There are also cities, such as Istanbul, in Turkey, that sit on both continents. Some people in Istanbul live in Asia and go to work in Europe.

A ferry across the Bosporus Strait transports people between Asia and Europe without leaving Istanbul!

Black Sea

EUROPE

Bosporus
Strait

Turkey

Istanbul

ASIA

Istanbul

Mediterranean
Sea

Many animals make their homes in towns and cities. These white storks nest on roofs in Spain. People like them because they keep insects and lizards out of people's homes.

CHAPTER 2

Wonderful Wildlife

Wild animals in Europe have had to cope with an expanding human population. Some animals live in areas that are hard for people to reach. Others have learned to live alongside humans. Many European species are related to those in North America. This is because millions of years ago Eurasia and North America were joined.

More than 10,000 wild red foxes live in the city of London.

Survival at Stake

Eastern gray squirrel

The red squirrel is Europe's native squirrel. But nowadays red squirrels are becoming rare. Why? Because of a newcomer, the Eastern gray squirrel. Gray squirrels traveled to Europe by stowing away on ships from North America. The two squirrels aren't at war with each other. But the gray squirrel carries a disease that makes red squirrels get sick or die.

In parts of England, the red squirrel is endangered.

At birth, Camargue (ka-MARG) horses are dark-colored. After a few years, they turn almost white.

Famous Wild Horses

A small, sturdy breed of wild horse lives in the Camargue region of southeast France. Its wide hooves are well adapted for the saltwater marshes that are its home. Some Camargue horses are now tame. However, many still run free—they live outdoors and never wear horseshoes.

A Lie About Lemmings

A false notion has given fame to Scandinavia's Norway lemming. That notion is that these animals willingly jump off cliffs to drown in the sea. The truth is that lemmings breed until they are too crowded in one area. Then thousands migrate to new areas to search for food. Sometimes they reach the edge of the sea. Lemmings are good swimmers, so they sometimes try to swim across as if the sea were a river. In the effort, many animals tire and drown.

The 1958 movie *Wild Wilderness* is often blamed for the myth of the cliff-jumping lemmings.

These local fishermen dock their boat at Positano, Italy.

European Fish

Herring, sturgeon, cod, tuna, and sardines are some of the important fish from Europe's waters. Caviar, or fish eggs, is also harvested. Caviar is famous for its high price. The most expensive caviar ever cost $700 for one ounce (28.3 grams). That's only a heaping spoonful!

This aqueduct was built by the Romans about 2,000 years ago in France. It was used to carry water to a nearby city.

CHAPTER 3

Ancient and Amazing

People have lived on the European continent for more than 700,000 years. However, European civilization can largely be traced to two ancient civilizations that were more recent. The earlier of these grew up about 3,000 years ago, in Greece. About 1,000 years later, ancient Rome rose to dominance. The influence and output of Greece and Rome are still seen all over Europe.

Pont du Gard is the highest aqueduct bridge ever built by the Romans.

Great Greeks

The ancient Greeks began the European tradition of **democracy**. They also studied science, mathematics, and **philosophy**. The most famous Greek philosopher was Socrates. He believed that babies know everything before they are born but forget it at birth.

The ancient Greeks produced finely painted pottery.

Scenes from the lives of gods and heroes were often depicted on pottery.

About 125 A.D., the Romans built Hadrian's Wall in England. The 73-mile-long wall protected them from invaders from Scotland.

Ruling Romans

The Romans **conquered** most of Europe, from England in the west to Turkey in the east. They greatly influenced European **architecture**, law, and poetry. Their language, Latin, is still used for many medical and scientific terms. Many Roman roads and buildings survive today. The empire, however, broke apart by about 500 A.D.

Dark Times

The years between 500 and 1400 in Europe are called the Middle Ages. Kings and queens ruled most of Europe, but life was not grand. Many Greek and Roman achievements were forgotten. The Catholic Church was the dominant force. Ordinary people were peasants, working on farms for landowners. Peasants lived in simple houses with no running water or toilets. Often, they didn't have the right to move away from their birthplace.

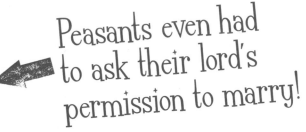

Peasants even had to ask their lord's permission to marry!

This painting shows a peasant woman carrying leeks.

Castles of Europe

Castles were very important in Europe in the Middle Ages. They were usually built for defense. To protect them from enemy attack, the walls were very thick. Castles were often built on hills or surrounded by a moat, or deep ditch. The moat was filled with water, or with sharp sticks, to stop the enemy. Royalty, **nobles**, and peasants lived within the castle walls in times of danger.

The Alcázar of Segovia, in Spain, is said to have inspired the Cinderella castle at Disney World, in Florida.

Rebirth

Beginning in the 1400s, European life began to change. The invention of the printing press meant that ideas and information could spread farther and faster. Europeans "rediscovered" ancient Greece and Rome, whose learning had been kept alive in the **Muslim** world. Europeans began to study philosophy, science, and mathematics again. They also began to explore the world. This period is called the Renaissance, which means "rebirth."

Leonardo da Vinci studied dead bodies to help him draw people realistically.

Italian artist and scientist Leonardo da Vinci (1452–1519) studied how people and machines worked.

Discovery and Takeover

In 1492, Christopher Columbus discovered America. Soon Europeans conquered this "New World." They sent home gold and furs. These riches sparked an Age of Exploration. Europeans conquered lands in Africa, Asia, Australia, and the Americas. In some places, they made the people into slaves. By the late 1800s, Europeans ruled most of the world.

Christopher Columbus landed first in the Bahamas. He gave the island of San Salvador its Spanish name.

Country in a City

Vatican City is a city that is also a country. That is, this inside another city. It is located within the city of Rome. The ruler of Vatican City is the Pope. He is also the head of the Catholic church. Vatican City is Europe's only theocracy. A theocracy is a country run by a religious leader.

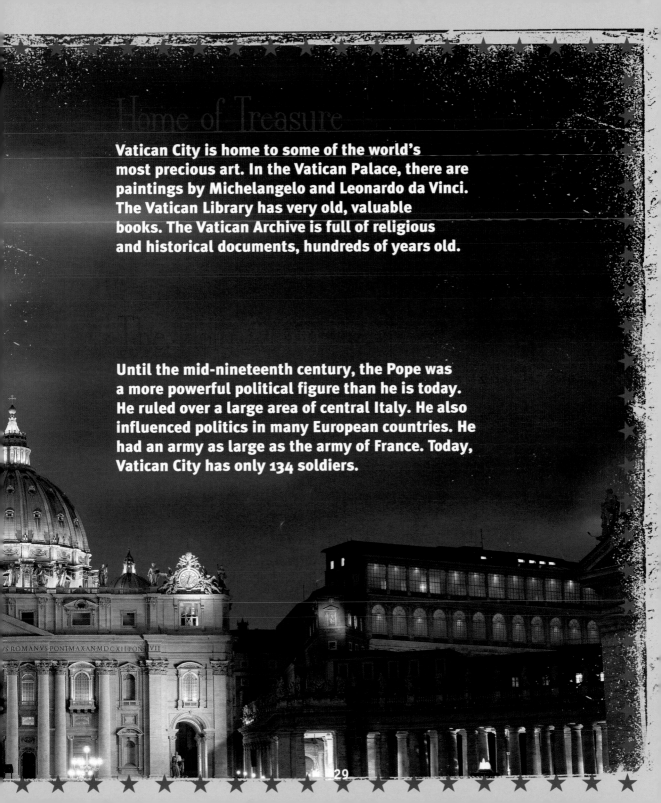

Home of Treasure

Vatican City is home to some of the world's
most precious art. In the Vatican Palace, there are
paintings by Michelangelo and Leonardo da Vinci.
The Vatican Library has very old, valuable
books. The Vatican Archive is full of religious
and historical documents, hundreds of years old.

Until the mid-nineteenth century, the Pope was
a more powerful political figure than he is today.
He ruled over a large area of central Italy. He also
influenced politics in many European countries. He
had an army as large as the army of France. Today,
Vatican City has only 134 soldiers.

This woman is making shell cases at a British weapons plant during World War I (1914–1918).

CHAPTER 4

Fights for Power

The twentieth century was marked by power struggles in Europe. By 1900, machines and technology had transformed life. Industry, rather than farming, drove economies. The nations of the world had become more interdependent. Conflicts within Europe began to spread beyond its borders. The twentieth century's two world wars started in Europe but changed the course of global history.

With men away at war, women took over many traditionally male jobs, such as working in factories.

Birth of the Soviet Union

For centuries, the poor of Russia suffered under **autocratic** rulers called czars. In 1917, Russia's czar was finally overthrown in a **revolution**. **Communists** took control. They promised a society where all wealth would be shared equally. The new country was called the Soviet Union. The Soviet Union was not a free country. People could go to prison or even be killed for saying something bad about the government.

For months, the czar and his family were held prisoner in their own palace.

Paying for the War

In World War I, Germany fought the United Kingdom, France, and Russia. This war was the first to be fought with tanks and airplanes. The death toll was horrific. Germany lost the war and was forced to accept responsibility for it. It had to give up land and pay damages. Many Germans felt unfairly treated. By the 1930s, many people were out of work. German money lost value. The country couldn't recover.

By the 1930s, German money was so worthless that children made kites out of it.

World War II (1939-1945)

In 1933, a man named Adolf Hitler came to power in Germany. He promised to make Germany powerful and wealthy again. Hitler and his allies built huge armies and in 1939 began to invade neighboring countries. By the summer of 1940, they had conquered most of Europe. By 1941, the United Kingdom, the United States, and the Soviet Union had joined forces to stop them. In 1945, after enormous losses on both sides, Hitler's army was finally defeated.

Time Line of Turbulence

1914–1918

About 15 million people die in World War I.

1917

The Russian Revolution leads to the birth of the Soviet Union.

Aftermath

The main powers that defeated Germany were the United Kingdom, the United States, and the Soviet Union. As Europe recovered after the war, the influence of those nations continued. Western Europe was mostly democratic, like the United Kingdom and the United States. In Eastern Europe, the Soviets set up Communist control. Germany was split into democratic West Germany and Communist East Germany. Its capital, Berlin, was divided into U.S., French, Soviet, and British zones.

1939–1945

About 60 million people die in World War II. Western Europe is no longer the center of world power.

1989

The Berlin Wall, symbol of divided Germany, is torn down. Germany is reunited.

Former West Germany

Former East Germany

CHAPTER 5

Today's Europeans

Europe has changed greatly in the last few decades. Beginning in 1989, Soviet control of eastern Europe fell apart. Many countries, such as Poland, regained their independence. Others, such as Slovakia, were born. Europe today has about 500 million people. Its birthrate is falling. However, its population is swelling with immigrants. Change is under way.

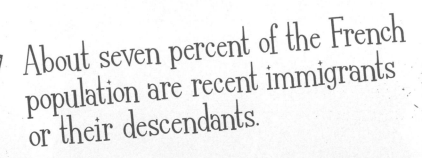

About seven percent of the French population are recent immigrants or their descendants.

Languages Galore

There are more than 35 native languages in Europe. These include Italian, English, and Latvian. Other languages, such as Vietnamese, have been introduced by immigrants. There are also more than 100 dialects spoken. A dialect is a variation of a major language and is usually spoken in a limited area.

The Romani people of Spain speak Spanish Caló.

May School in rural Ireland is helping to save the country's native language. Almost all the subjects are taught in Gaelic.

Saving Languages

Europe has many micro-languages—native languages spoken by a small number of people. Some of these began to die out because people used more widely spoken languages, such as English. Today, there are efforts to bring these native languages back into use. In some countries, children learn them at school. In others, there are micro-language television programs.

Euro Power

In 1957, six countries in Europe joined to create a European Economic Community. They wanted to make it easier to buy and sell between different countries. In 2007, that little club of six turned into the European Union (EU) of 27 countries. EU countries share laws about work and finance. Europeans sometimes complain that the EU makes a lot of silly rules. Once, the EU tried to make a law about how curvy bananas should be!

Most EU countries use a common currency, the euro. Euro paper money looks the same in all EU countries.

© BCE ECB EZB EKT EKP 2002

5 EURO
EYPΩ

KT EKP 2002

EURO

Freedom of Movement

The European Union has an agreement that allows Europeans more freedom to move around within Europe. In the past, the citizens of one country could not live and work in another without a permit. Today, citizens of EU countries are free to live and work anywhere in the union.

A tunnel has been dug under the English Channel between England and France. Some people commute between Paris and London on a high-speed train.

In London, England, the Gherkin skyscraper sits alongside buildings that are hundreds of years old.

Europe's Future

Europeans are surrounded every day by evidence of their long history. At the same time, Europe is one of the most technologically advanced parts of the world. Computers and castles are both parts of everyday life. People from all over the world now live in the cities of Europe. The transformation of Europe is in progress. ★

True Statistics

Number of countries: 48

Largest castle: Prague Castle in the Czech Republic

Tallest mountain: Mount Elbrus in the Ural Mountains

Largest city: Moscow–8.3 million people

Northernmost cities: Hammerfest, Norway and Honningsvåg, Norway

Longest river: The Volga flows 2,194 miles (3,531 kilometers) through Russia

Oldest amusement park (still in operation): Tivoli Gardens, Copenhagen, Denmark (1843)

Did you find the truth?

F Europe's birthrate is increasing rapidly.

T In Venice, Italy, canals take the place of some streets.

Resources

Books

Corbishley, Mike. *The Middle Ages* (Cultural Atlas for Young People). New York: Chelsea House Publishers, 2007.

Day, Nancy. *Your Travel Guide to Renaissance Europe* (Passport to History). Minneapolis: Runestone Press, 2001.

Fowler, Allan. *Europe* (Rookie Read-About Geography). Danbury, CT: Children's Press, 2002.

Harvey, Miles. *The Fall of the Soviet Union* (Cornerstones of Freedom). Danbury, CT: Children's Press, 1995.

Lace, William. *Building History—The Vatican* (Building History). San Diego: Lucent Books, 2003.

Moore, Jo Ellen. *Europe*. Monterey, CA: Evan-Moor Educational Publishers, 1999.

Scott, Janine. *The Two Great Wars* (Shockwave: Social Studies). New York: Children's Press, 2008.

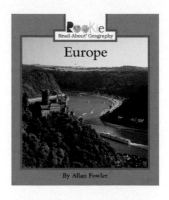

Organizations and Web Sites

Ancient Civilizations
www.kidspast.com
This Web site offers information and games about ancient civilizations, the Renaissance, and the Middle Ages.

European History and the European Union
www.eurunion.org/infores/teaching/Young/EUYoungPeople.htm
Learn more about Europe with these photographs, activities, and games.

Places to Visit

Louvre Museum
99, rue de Rivoli
Paris 75058, France
+33 (0) 140 20 5317
www.louvre.fr/llv/commun/
home.jsp?bmLocale=en
One of Europe's great museums, the Louvre has legendary works such as the *Mona Lisa*.

The Metropolitan Museum of Art
1000 Fifth Avenue
New York, NY 10028-0198
(212) 535 7710
www.metmuseum.org
See art and artifacts from every period of European history, including ancient Greece and Rome.

Important Words

architecture (AR-ki-tek-chur) – the study of designing
  buildings

autocratic (aw-tuh-CRAT-ik) – said of a situation in which
  a person rules with unlimited authority and power

canal (kuh-NAL) – a passage that is dug across land
  to connect bodies of water

Communist (KOM-yuh-nist) – one who believes in organizing
  a country so that all the property belongs to the government
  or community, and the profits of production are shared

conquer (KON-kur) – to take control of a place and its people

democracy (di-MOK-ruh-see) – a form of government in which
  the people choose their leaders in competitive elections

latitude (LAT-uh-tood) – a position north or south of the
  equator

Muslim (MUHZ-luhm) – a follower of the religion of Islam

noble (NOH-buhl) – a person born into wealth and
  high status

philosophy (fuh-LOSS-uh-fee) – the basic beliefs, ideas,
  and attitudes of an individual or group

revolution (rev-uh-LOO-shuhn) – an uprising by the people
  of a country that changes the way the country is governed

Index

Page numbers in **bold** indicate illustrations

About the Author

Sandra Newman is a novelist and professor living in New York City. She is the author or co-author of four books for adults, both fiction and nonfiction. She lived in Europe for 20 years, in countries including England, Russia, Germany, France, the Czech Republic, and the Ukraine.

PHOTOGRAPHS: Big Stock Photo (© Paul Merrett, p. 9; p. 15; p. 40); Briony Hill (p. 4; p. 22); Getty Images (front cover; p. 30; pp. 32–33); Ingram Image Library (back cover; p. 10); iStockphoto (©Fanelie Rosier, p. 17; p. 35); Jake Henderson (p. 12); Photo New Zealand (age fotostock, p. 18); Photodisc (p. 43); Photolibrary (p. 12; p. 23; pp. 28–29; p. 41); Stock.XCHNG (p. 3; snake, p. 5; Eastern gray squirrel, p. 16; p. 34; p. 42); Stockxpert (back cover; p. 13; red squirrel, p. 16; ©Elena Elisseeva, p. 20; pp. 34–35); Tranz (Corbis, p. 6; p. 19; pp. 24–27; pp. 38–39; Photoshot, p. 14; Reuters, p. 36)